Carefree Summers and Smoky Clothes

Stories of Mischief and Mayhem

Sean D Sweet

Acknowledgements

Acknowledgement to my childhood friend **John Shelley**, whose Chopper bike proudly features on the front cover of this book.
John was taken from us far too soon but will be remembered fondly by all of us who were lucky enough to share those carefree days with him.

Further acknowledgement to Mam, Dad, my sister Lesley, and my brother Phillip, who lived through all my mischief and mayhem — with patience, laughter, and the occasional flying Scholl sandal.

Thank you all for the memories that became these stories.

Sean D Sweet

Introduction

My name is Sean Sweet, and I was born in 1966 in Gateshead, Tyne and Wear. My paternal grandfather was a successful local businessman who owned and ran a ceramic tiling company. We lived in nearby Birtley, in a grand home called Birtley Springs.

Sadly, when I was around six years old, my parents, Rosemary and Bill, separated and divorced. Although my mother had married into the wealthy Sweet family—millionaires at the time—she left the marriage with nothing. My mam, along with my sister Lesley, my brother Phillip, and myself moved to Sulgrave in Washington.

Going from life in the Manor House to a council house was a huge shock for mam. As children, we adapted quickly—especially me as I was so young. We only stayed in Washington for about a year before moving again, this time to a council house in Chester-le-Street, where we would live for many years.

My dad eventually remarried a woman named Linda, who had two sons, Steven and Nigel from her first marriage. They went on and had a child of their own, Helen my younger sister.

This book is a collection of short stories — my true adventures and mishaps, experienced between my home in Chester-le-Street and my dad's caravan at Beadnell on the Northumberland Coast. I hope you enjoy reading them as much as I enjoyed living (and surviving!) them.

Table of Contents

Acknowledgements

Introduction

Chapter 1 Sliced Tomatoes and Comics

Chapter 2 The Cowboy Gun

Chapter 3 The Truck Tyre

Chapter 4 Farming Outlook

Chapter 5 Cowpat and Picnic at Sea

Chapter 6 Brown Ale and Broken Bricks

Chapter 7 The Garage Den

Chapter 8 Bubblegum and Swan Vestas

Chapter 9 The Railway Station

Chapter 10 The Commando Club

Chapter 11 Away with the Tide

Chapter 12 The Ouija Board

Chapter 13 Pud and the Durex

Chapter 14 The Tent

Chapter 15 Dallas and the Wallpaper Paste

Chapter 16 The Essoldo

Chapter 17 Kermit and the Coppers Boot

Chapter 18 Cherry Tree Road and the Washing Machine

Chapter 1

Sliced Tomato and Comics

Every six weeks meant one thing: - time at our caravan in Beadnell. The days were glorious — all sunburnt adventures and freedom by the sea. But the evenings? Boring beyond belief!

Once the sun dipped, the fun dipped with it. The caravan TV only worked when Dad's car battery had enough juice (which wasn't often), and the hiss of the gas lamps was about as exciting as it got. When Dad and Linda headed off to the village pub, my brother Phil and stepbrother Steven were left in charge.

That sounded fine in theory — until they invented "the game\".

The rules were simple: Nigel and I had to sit on the floor, knees to our chests, eyes glued to the telly, and most importantly — not make a sound.

If one of us so much as giggled, a tin coffee tray would be launched like a frisbee straight at our shins. Didn't matter who laughed — we both got it. And believe me, those trays stung.

The more we tried not to laugh, the harder it was to stay quiet. Our bruised shins became the battle scars of every Beadnell summer.

Earlier that evening, we'd sat down for tea. Linda had made her usual ham salad sandwiches — and, to my horror, they were infested with the devil's ingredient - sliced tomato. I hated tomato. The smell, the texture, the slime — just looking at it made me gag.

When I said I didn't like it, Linda gave me that look and said, "Don't be silly, it's only tomato. Eat it." So I did what any self-respecting kid would do — I started sneaking the slices out. Unfortunately, Nigel spotted me.

"Mam! Sean's taking the tomato out of his sandwiches!" he squealed. Linda spun around, furious. "That's it! Leave the table — no dessert for you."

And that was that. No Mr Kipling apple pies. No warm custard. Just me, half a sandwich, and a burning desire for revenge.

Later, once Dad and Linda had left for the pub, Phil and Steven announced, "Right, you two — pyjamas on. You can watch telly, but no noise."

Nigel was quick to change, all smug and innocent, while I was in the bedroom hatching my plan. Revenge. Sweet, silent revenge!

I found an old pair of football socks and stuffed three or four comics down each leg — Roy of the Rovers, The Beano — anything I could find. My shins were armoured. I pulled my dressing gown over the top, hiding the evidence, and strutted into the living room like a knight in shining armour.

We took our usual positions — knees up, mouths shut, and Porridge came on. Within minutes, we were both struggling not to laugh.

Then it happened. I cracked. A laugh burst out before I could stop it.

The tin tray came flying.

CLANG!

It hit my legs — and… nothing. Not a hint of pain. I faked a wince, rubbed my shins, and moaned dramatically while, beside me, poor Nigel howled in genuine agony.

A few minutes later, it happened again. I laughed, the tray flew, and once more, I felt glorious nothing.

I kept it going — tray after tray, laugh after laugh — until my secret mission was complete.

No Mr Kipling pies. No custard. But that night, for the first time in Beadnell holiday history, I went to bed grinning…

…and bruise-free.

Chapter 2

The Cowboy Gun

Most young lads love toy guns and I was no exception. I'm not sure when or who bought it for me, but I was the proud owner of a shiny silver cowboy gun with a red plastic handle.

The gun took a roll of red caps which fed through the hammer and made a loud bang when you pulled the trigger — leaving a small cloud of smoke and that lovely smell of sulphur. I'd buy those caps on a Saturday with my pocket money from the newsagent and toy shop called Greeners in the middle of Chester-le-Street Front Street.

Mam would hate it when I got those caps. All anyone would hear was me pretending to have a gunfight with imaginary opponents and sneaking up and firing at anyone who happened to be nearby. Eventually the toy gun was resigned to the toy box where most of my toys ended up — not totally forgotten, just resting until my imagination brought them back to life.

Months went by and I hadn't even thought once about the cowboy gun. One morning I heard the old lady across the road asking the postman if he had any spare elastic bands, and to my astonishment watched the postman reach into his bag and pull out a huge handful — every colour, every length and thickness. He handed them to Doris and went about his day.

I wanted some. The next day I caught up with the postman on the way to school.

"Excuse me, Postie — do you have any spare elastic bands?" I asked.

He immediately reached into his post bag and handed me a wriggling handful of elastic bands. "Thanks!" I shouted, running off with my new treasure.

I decided I would collect elastic bands. Why? I had no idea — it just seemed a good plan. Every time I saw the postman I asked him, until one day he didn't even wait to be asked. At the sight of me he'd plunge his hand into his bag and pass me a big bunch of elastic bands.

One Saturday afternoon, cartoons finished, I was bored so out came my collection of elastic bands. I had an idea: I'd make an elastic rope. I got to work looping all the big, strong bands together and after a while had a rope about four feet long. Now what to do? Let's test its strength, I thought. I'd tie something on one end and see what would happen.

After looking through the toy box for something suitable I spotted the cowboy gun. That's it I thought. I tied one end of the elastic rope through the trigger loop and the other end to the dining room door. I stretched the elastic rope across the dining room and up the hallway. The rope was strained to its limit; the cowboy gun was ready to launch — and launch it did.

Travelling at break-neck speed, it shot down the hallway, around the corner into the dining room, followed by an almighty bang — a bang so loud I was terrified to look. When I did, I got the shock of my life. The metal gun had hit the door with such force it had gone straight through, leaving a hole the size of a tennis ball.

I knew immediately I was in big trouble. Mam didn't have much money and repairing a door was something she couldn't afford.

I decided I would hide the hole and, if she was in a good mood, tell her about it later. I pushed the door back against the frame and put the washing basket in front of it. That didn't go to plan — Mam moved the basket within minutes of being in the house. She knew it was me, not just from the look on my face but because who else could destroy a door without trying?

Grounded for two weekends and no more elastic bands.

Chapter 3

The Truck Tyre

Every other weekend I went to stay with my Dad and his second wife, Linda. They lived in Low Fell, just outside Gateshead, with her two sons, Nigel and Steven.

I loved going to stay at Dad's — it was like a holiday every other weekend — and on a Saturday we would have what I called a party tea: sandwiches, cakes, jelly and custard.

Me Mam said Linda only made teas like that because she couldn't cook if her life depended on it, but nevertheless, I loved those party teas.

I would finish school on a Friday and run all the way home to collect my bag, which I'd packed the previous night, then catch the bus to Low Fell. Every weekend at my Dad's house was an adventure — different from my weekends in Chester-le-Street.

Most Saturday mornings we went to the cinema. They would play short films and cartoons, and it was called the Saturday Morning Cinema Club.

One Saturday morning, Nigel and I had gone to the cinema as usual and were being our usual mischievous selves, throwing popcorn at the seats in front. Someone went and grassed us up to the manager and we were asked to leave. That was it — we'd spent our pocket money and were now forced to walk the streets.

We walked up toward the Rugby Club. I liked the Rugby Club — they often had open days and fetes where you could buy sweets and cakes. Once they even had local celebrity Kathy Secker, who read the Tyne Tees News, to open the fete. She was selling kisses for 50p each. Even at the early age of nine, I thought a 50p kiss from that gorgeous woman was worth every penny. Eagerly I joined the queue and noticed that the kiss was just a peck on the cheek. Stuff that I thought — if I'm paying 50p, I'm having it on the lips.

When it came to my turn, she leaned in and offered her left cheek, but I whipped my head round and planted one right on her lips!

"You cheeky little bugger!" she said, laughing.

I never forgot that kiss, and every time I passed the Rugby Club, I thought of Kathy Secker.

Anyway on with the story. We arrived at the Rugby Club but nothing was on so we started making our way down towards the Fell. We crossed the High Street and made our way through the private housing estate to the rear of the shops. On route, we came across a large tyre and immediately started pushing it down the road.

At the top of the housing estate there was an alleyway that ran for about a quarter of a mile — a straight tarmac path with concrete steps every so often as the bank got steeper that eventually came out on the road next to the Nine Pins pub.

We strategically positioned the tyre at the entrance to the alley and set it rolling. At first it hit the fence on one side and started to wobble as if it was going to stop — but it didn't. Instead, it picked up speed and cleared a full set of steps.

We ran alongside it for a bit, cheering it on like lunatics, until it disappeared out of sight.

About thirty seconds later, we heard the screech of brakes. We looked at each other with eyes wide, and did what any brave nine-year-olds would do - we legged it and said nothing to anyone.

Later, we found out the tyre had narrowly missed hitting a car, but it had smashed straight through a small garden wall opposite the alley.

From that day on, every time we walked past that alley, we made sure to do it very casually — hands in pockets, eyes to the front. We were just two innocent lads out for a walk!

Chapter 4

Farming Outlook

It was Monday night and I was at the youth centre when I noticed a sign-up sheet on the noticeboard. The heading read Tyne Tees TV – Farm Visit.

It wasn't so much the words Farm Visit that caught my attention — it was Tyne Tees TV. An actual chance of being on television and being famous! I immediately put my name down and wished hard as only some of the names would be chosen.

A week later the successful applicant list went up, and to my disbelief my name was on it!

The visit was scheduled for a Saturday afternoon at the end of June. The day came and we all gathered outside the youth centre waiting for the coach. It arrived and off we went — a bus loaded with excited kids heading to a dairy farm near Bishop Auckland.

When we got there we were marched across a field to where a camera crew was set up and were filming a herd of cows. The presenter came over and explained that anyone who wanted to ask a question could do so on camera. Perfect I thought. I started working on my question — and soon I had the perfect one - "How many pints of milk does the average cow produce?" Brilliant. I was ready.

The presenter began talking about the farm, and then came our turn to ask the questions.

"Does anyone have any questions?" he asked.

The camera panned to a lad called Tony. "At what age do the cows start producing milk?" he asked.

"Good question," said the farmer. "The cow produces milk almost immediately after giving birth."

Then a girl called Sharon jumped up, arm straight as an arrow."What is the cow's diet? Do they only eat grass?"

"Another good question," said the farmer. "Cows can eat 100% grass, but ours live on a mix of grass and grains."

The camera moved down the line. My stomach tightened — my turn was coming. But before I could speak, a tall lad shoved forward, arm in the air. The farmer pointed to him.

"How many pints of milk does the average cow produce?" he said.

My heart sank. That was my question!

"Very good question, son," said the farmer. "The average cow produces twenty-four pints a day."

I froze. My mind raced — think, think, think! My hand was still up, and now the camera was on me. The farmer nodded.

"What's your question, son?"

And out it came, completely unplanned, **"Have you got any black and white cows?"**

"Well son," the farmer replied patiently, "we don't have any black and white cows — that particular breed are Holstein-Friesians. We have a mix of Jersey and Guernsey cows."

I nodded as if I understood, my head was swimming and inside I was dying.

The next day I told everyone it had been boring and that I hadn't been on TV. But the other kids who were there made sure everyone knew about the black and white cows.

The programme wasn't being aired for another month, so I tried to forget about it and get on with daily life. Until one day when Max, who ran the youth centre, put up a big reminder in reception:

DON'T MISS FARMING OUTLOOK THIS SUNDAY!

That Sunday afternoon, Mam, Lesley, Phill and I gathered round the telly. My moment came - "Have you got any black and white cows?"

Mam said I was fantastic. Lesley said nothing. Phill buried his face in a cushion and laughed and laughed.

The credits hadn't even finished when the phone rang. Mam answered:

"Hello, Chester-le-Street 888864."

A loud voice shouted down the line:

"Have you got any black and white cows?"

It went on for days. Mam said she knew who it was and would speak to their parents, but I told her to leave it — they'd get sick of the joke eventually.

I never watched Farming Outlook again. It had all been too embarrassing.

Granda said it was character-building — and at least I'd learned some interesting facts about cows!

My sister Lesley at Beadnell outside our family Caravan.

Chapter 5

Cow Pat and Picnic at Sea

We woke up to the sound of rain belting down on the caravan roof.

"Come on, you two — it's after eight! Get up, you need to do your jobs!"

Another day at Beadnell Links during the summer holidays. Phil and I trudged off to the toilet block carrying the plastic wee bucket between us — urine sloshing onto our hands as we shared the job, one on either side. We emptied it at the sluice and headed back for the next job.

"We're out of milk and bread. Can one of you go to the village and get milk, bread, and a newspaper?"

The rain had stopped and the sun was coming out, so Nigel and I said we'd go.

We took the shortcut through the cow field on the way to the village, stopping to throw stones into the pond. Then I spotted it — the biggest, freshest cow pat I'd ever seen.

I pulled a large flat stone from the dry-stone wall and shouted to Nigel. When he was at the perfect distance, I angled the stone and threw it straight into the middle of the cow pat.

The result was far worse than I'd imagined. Nigel was covered in cow shit — head to toe. He burst into tears and ran back toward the caravan.

I carried on to the village, bought the milk, bread, and newspaper, and headed back — proud of my shopping but slightly nervous about my reception.

Linda was waiting at the caravan door with Dad.

"That was disgusting, what you did to Nigel," she snapped. "Your dad's taking you home."

They'd already packed my bag. I got in the car without a word.

Dad drove in silence until we reached Chathill, then pulled over.

"Listen, son — you need to start behaving yourself."

I told him how sorry I was. He sighed, turned the car around, and headed back.

"How's Nigel?" I asked.

Dad gave a small smile. "He's alright. Had to change his clothes and have a shower."

When we got back, Linda was still frosty, but after a while she softened.

"Go on, you two — get yourselves out to play," she said, handing us a bag. "There's a picnic."

We walked along the beach for a while, poking at a dead seagull with a stick — as young, inquisitive boys do, until we reached the area where the sailing boats were moored.

The tide was out, and the yachts and small boats were resting on the sand. We wandered among them, having a look around until we spotted a cabin door swinging open on one of the yachts.

Exploration time! I bunked Nigel up first and passed him the bag of sandwiches. Then he helped pull me aboard.

It was fantastic — our own private cabin! We sat there eating sandwiches and drinking pop, and in a drawer we found a packet of Top Trumps. We played a few rounds, talking and laughing, completely losing track of time. Then we noticed something strange — the cabin seemed to be swaying.

We opened the door and climbed onto the deck. To our horror the tide was fully in and the yacht was now floating in deep water. Nigel started to cry.

"Don't worry," I said. "I'll swim and tow us in."

I had no idea the yacht was anchored — I didn't have a chance in hell of moving it! I slipped into the water, positioned myself between the mooring ropes, and started swimming. No matter how hard I tried, it wouldn't move.

Nigel was still crying and I couldn't even get back on board — the sides were too high.

"HELP!" we both started shouting.

A crowd had began to gather on the harbour, watching the two young boys on the boat. Someone went to call for help.

Before long the Seahouses inshore lifeboat arrived and pulled us aboard, taking us safely back to shallow water.

Meanwhile, Dad and Linda had been out for a walk and saw the crowd on the harbour. They stopped to see what was going on — and their jaws dropped when they spotted Nigel and me being hauled off the yacht by the lifeboat crew.

I was freezing. Nigel was traumatised again, this was his second ordeal of the day.

What an adventure! Were summers always going to be this good?!

Chapter 6

Brown Ale and Broken Bricks

As with many of my childhood stories, this was one that happened during the 1970's — approximately 1974,

At the top of Co-operative Street there was a row of houses that had been earmarked for demolition. Of course, as 10-year-old boys we knew nothing of these plans and Neil Petrie, Colin Winter, Raymond Gedling, Neil Wilkinson and myself saw this as a chance to explore.

One of the houses had an attic room which we commandeered as our clubhouse.

We decided that the clubhouse needed items to furnish it. In our excitement what we needed to furnish the club with became misunderstood. We had no idea!

I supplied a bottle of Brown Ale which I had taken from the fridge at home. This was placed on the mantelpiece at the clubhouse, where it sat like a religious deity. Once this was in place, all club members were required to supply an item which would improve the clubhouse.

Can't remember exactly who supplied what, but obviously no clubhouse was complete without a classroom thermometer, a rack of permanent coloured markers, several board games, and books.

It wasn't long before our school teacher noticed the disappearance of classroom items. A message went out in the school assembly that the culprit or culprits stealing school property would be caught and punished. We met at break time and decided not to take another thing from the classroom and swore to each other not to mention this to anyone.

Although we didn't take any more items from the classroom, Neil Petrie decided we needed a set of cutlery for the clubhouse and proceeded to gather two or three sets from the school canteen, tucking them into the belt of his trousers. After we had finished our lunch and made our way to stack our dirty plates, there was suddenly an almighty clatter as three sets of cutlery made their way down Neil's trouser leg and onto the tiled floor of the dinner hall.

"What's going on?" shouted one of the dinner nannies.

Neil quickly came up with an explanation, blaming me — saying I had tucked them into his jumper as a prank. To our amazement, we were told not to be silly and to leave the dinner hall.

The Easter holidays had arrived, and we had been spending a lot of time at the clubhouse. One particular day during the holidays we could hear lots of noise outside the house. To our surprise, when we looked out the window, a large area in front of the row of houses had been cordoned off, and two or three pieces of heavy plant equipment were in place, including a crane with a huge wrecking ball.

As we peered out the window in astonishment, and I suppose fear, one of the group of local people who had gathered to see the demolition spotted us.

"Stop! There are kids in that house!"

There was a big commotion outside as people rushed to stop the wrecking ball from demolishing the building — and further commotion inside the house as we ran down the stairs as fast as we could.

The cordon and heavy machinery had been set up at the front of the house, so the obvious escape was through the kitchen, out the back door, over the wall of the back yard, and leg it to the top of the lane. We got to the top of the lane and crept around the corner, looking back towards the front of the houses to see what was happening.

It was at this point we realised Peche (Neil Petrie) had not come out of the house. As we all looked down towards the houses, to our amazement the front door of the house we had been in opened and Peche stepped out. Not batting an eyelid he walked through the workmen and the crowds of people who had gathered and up to the top of the lane where we were all crouching down hiding.

We sat and waited, and after about 30 minutes the houses had been searched and the all-clear was given. We watched as our beloved clubhouse and other houses were demolished.

Well, it had been fun while it lasted. The clubhouse was gone. We were gutted, but it had been exciting — and if we could find another clubhouse…

"I CAN GET ANOTHER BOTTLE OF BROWN ALE!"

Chapter 7

The Garage Den

I'm guessing it was sometime around 1975. I lived with my mam and my older brother and sister, Lesley and Phillip, in a three-bedroom council house in Chester-le-Street.

Like many small boys, I loved building camps and dens. Martin Gardner lived next door but one to us. One particular Saturday we decided to build a camp in our garage, which was mostly used for storing bikes, old furniture, and a couple of bed bases.

Didn't take long before we'd built ourselves a little den, made from the two bed bases and an old tabletop. Armed with a handful of comics and a candle for light, we shut ourselves in the garage and crawled inside.

We sat there for a while, reading comics by candlelight. When boredom set in, we decided to see how the hessian material on the bottom of the bed bases would burn.

Well — it burned great.

Martin lit it, I patted it out. Lit it, patted it out. We kept that up for a few minutes until, on the last go, Martin lit it and the flames grew too fierce for me to handle. We scrambled out of the den, threw open the garage door, and ran up the path shouting for my sister — the only one home. Phillip was out with his mates, and Mam was at Chester-le-Street Hospital, where she worked as a nurse.

"LESLEY! There's a fire in the garage!" I shouted.

"You little shit!" she yelled back, grabbing a dish full of dirty dishwater and charging down the path. Smoke was already pouring from the open garage door, but after a few more dishes and buckets of water, Lesley had it under control. The fire was out.

When Mam came home from work, Lesley wasted no time grassing me up.

"That little bugger and his mate have been lighting fires in the garage — burnt one of the old bed bases!"

Mam wasn't happy. I got sent to bed early.

I woke in the early hours of Sunday morning to find my brother's bed empty. We shared a room, and it was unusual for him not to be there. I got up and wandered into Mam's room. Her bed was empty too, and the whole room was lit up by flashing blue light.

I crept to the window and with trepidation lifted the net curtain.

Holy shit. The street was full of people and firemen, a whole fire engine sat strategically right outside. Even in the dark, the blue lights revealed thick black smoke pouring from our garage and the one next door. On our neighbour's drive was their car — clearly pulled from the garage — still smoking, its windows shattered.

As I stood frozen at the window, Mam, standing outside in her dressing gown beside a fireman, looked up and saw me. She pointed, said something to the fireman, who clenched his fist and shook it toward me like thunder.

I dived back into bed and hid under the blankets, praying it was all just a bad dream. Of course, it wasn't.

The next day told the story clear enough: both garage roofs had collapsed. On the drives lay twisted wreckage — bikes, old furniture, bed bases, and that tabletop that had once been the roof of our den. Next door's car was ruined, its paint bubbled and blistered, its windows blackened and cracked.

I was grounded for a long time after that — but it never quite cured my fascination with fire!

My brother Phill (left) my sister Lesley (right) and me centre.

Me, Lesley & Phill outside our family home in Birtley.

(Left) me, Lesley & Phill.

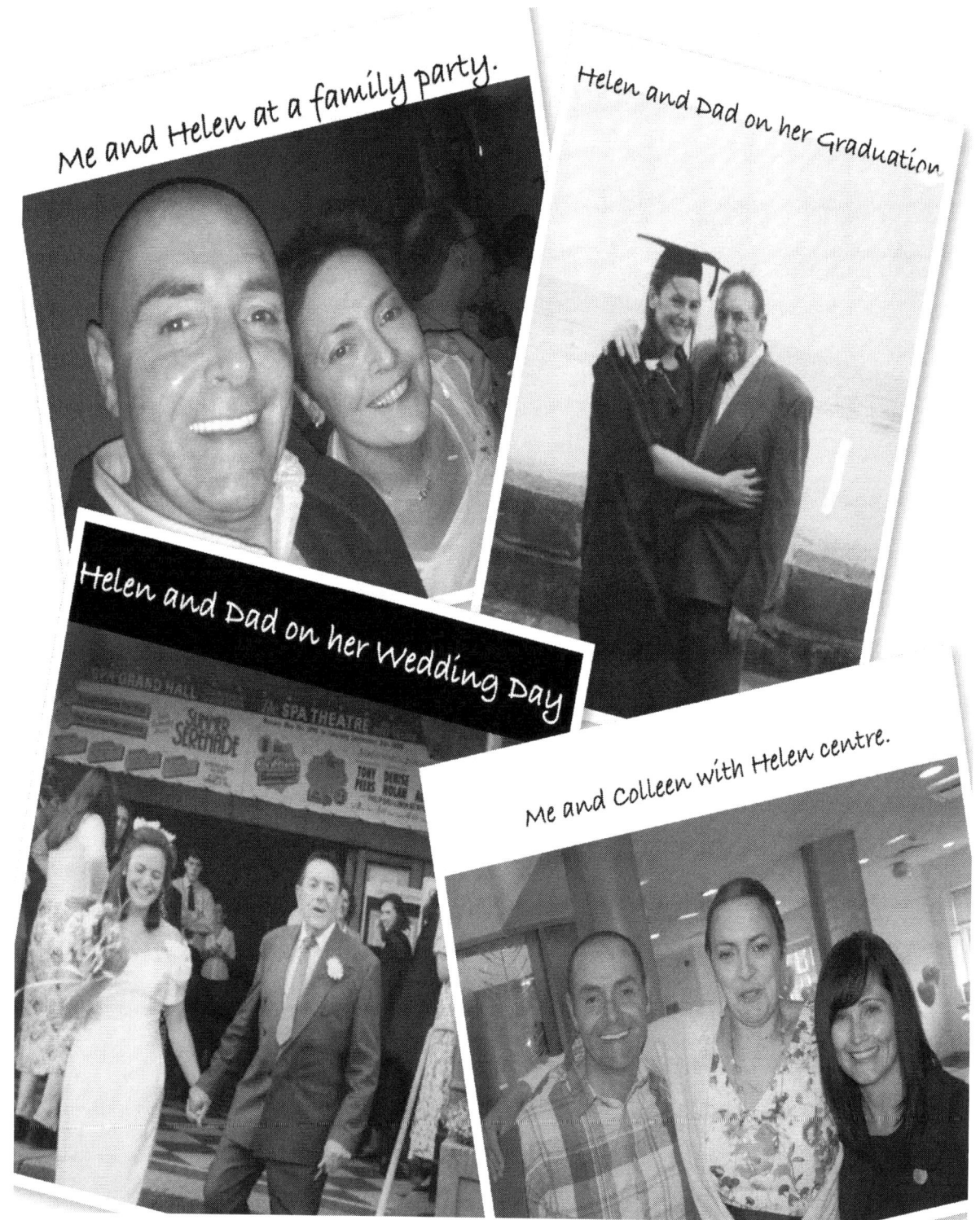

(Below) me and my brother Phill 1968 at Beadnell Links.

(Above) me and my brother Phill outside the garage Deleval 1980.

Holidays with Mam 🩶

Chapter 8

Bubble Gum and Swan Vestas

It was the summer of 1975, and the six weeks' holidays had just begun. We'd travelled from Gateshead to Beadnell Links — a caravan site where my dad had a static van.

Dad told me and my stepbrother to go and play while he unpacked the car. Off we went, pocket money in hand, heading straight for the campsite shop.

We bought a load of Bazooka bubble gum, and with my change I picked up a box of Swan Vestas matches.

We wandered off toward the sand dunes where we came across a discarded ICI blue plastic bag. I showed Nigel how, if you set plastic on fire, it dripped to the ground like little bombs. We wrapped bits of it around a couple of sticks, struck a few matches, and created our own flaming torches.

Now, the weather had been hot for weeks and the dunes were tinder dry. Yes — you've guessed it — within seconds the dunes were alight, flames racing across the sand faster than we could move.

We tried to stamp it out, but it was no good.

"Run, Nigel!" I shouted, and we legged it back to the caravan.

Dad was outside, unpacking boxes of bedding and clothes, and didn't see us sneaking inside. We dived into the bedroom and closed the door.

It wasn't long before we heard shouting and the clanging of metal — the fire alarm triangle being struck to warn the campers. I peeked through the caravan curtain and saw people running with buckets of water toward the thick black smoke rolling off the dunes.

Then came the loud click of the bedroom door. Dad stood there, red-faced, eyes blazing.

"I bloody knew it! Fire, fire, bloody fire — that's all you think about!" he roared.

The fire was eventually put out, but not before it scorched a good stretch of the dunes.

Needless to say, we were grounded, confined to the caravan for nearly a week and warned not to breathe a word to anyone. If we did, Dad said we'd be sent to the cottage homes! The cottage homes were a well-known children's residential home and neither of us wanted to go there!

Me, Lesley and Phill outside our family home in Birtley

Chapter 9

The Railway Station

It was November 1976, and Pud, Raymond and I were walking around the streets up to no good as usual.

At the bottom of Bullion Lane, just underneath the railway bridge was a patch of waste ground. This wasteland was the local dumping ground, but often with exciting items that young boys could turn into a plaything. As we passed by, we noticed a few new items that had been flytipped onto the land. To any young lad this was to be investigated, and we walked over to have a look at what there was. We were confronted by an old pram and a few bags of hardened cement. Disappointment fell upon us but soon vanished when I put my hand into my pocket and pulled out a box of matches.

As you will now have discovered, I was mesmerised and fascinated by fire. Unfortunately this obsession always seemed to end in trouble!

Temptation was too much. Just as I was attempting to set fire to the pram, my sister walked past and shouted, "You better get your arse up home me Mam has been looking for you!"

For a split second I did think about listening to her, but I was a young boy and had more exciting ideas on my mind. For a split moment I did think about going home but this thought was short lived. The burning of the pram was more interesting! I was transfixed with starting the fire, but no matter how hard I tried the material was too wet and even with my perseverance, wouldn't burn. What a disappointment!

Getting no results from the pram, Pud suddenly remembered and told us that there were lots of cardboard boxes at the back of the Railway Station. I had the matches, and we now had combustible material, what harm could be done?! Off we went.

Stacked behind the Railway Station were lots of cardboard boxes leaning against the wall of the old storerooms. By now each of us had a small box of matches so we set about lighting small corners of the boxes, just to see what would happen. Small burning corners could easily be put out and we weren't hurting anyone.

Amongst the boxes Raymond found an old brush head, he lit it and it blazed like the Olympic torch. He held it high! We followed him around like we were part of the Olympics. Unfortunately, very quickly the heat became too intense for him to hold onto the torch. So quickly in fact that he launched it into the already burning pile of cardboard!

Within minutes the boxes were all ablaze and the flames licked upwards towards the guttering of the Railway Station storerooms.

For a few seconds we stood looking at the fire with admiration and then the realisation of what we had done set in! "Leg it", I shouted to the others. We ran under the bridge and all the way home without stopping.

Next day at school, everyone was talking about the fire, and we were getting really worried. The three of us talked about what would happen if they found out it was us and discussed if we should run away from home. Unfortunately what we didn't realise was that we were directly below Mr Bonnie the headmaster's office, and the window was open and he heard every word. We were all summoned to his office.

Of course, we all denied it at first but soon the evidence against us was building. It didn't help that several kids from our school had seen us running away with black faces covered in soot. We were the talk of the school and beyond!

Mr Bonnie contacted our parents. He asked if they had seen the front page article of the Journal. It clearly outlined that on the previous evening the Chester le Street Railway Station had been burnt down by arsonists. Mr Bonnie informed our parents that he had reason to believe it was three boys, who were now all in his presence and one of whom was me!

My mam didn't need evidence, she knew it had my MO all over it! She knew exactly who those arsonists were.

When school finished, I came out of the gate and across the road and there was my Mam waiting for me with a face like thunder. She marched me home, and as soon as we got in, she called the Police. Yes, my own mam grassed us up – all three of us! Due to our age we each received a Police caution. This is one experience that I never want to encounter ever again! It never stopped my fasciation with fire but did curtail my exploits with it.

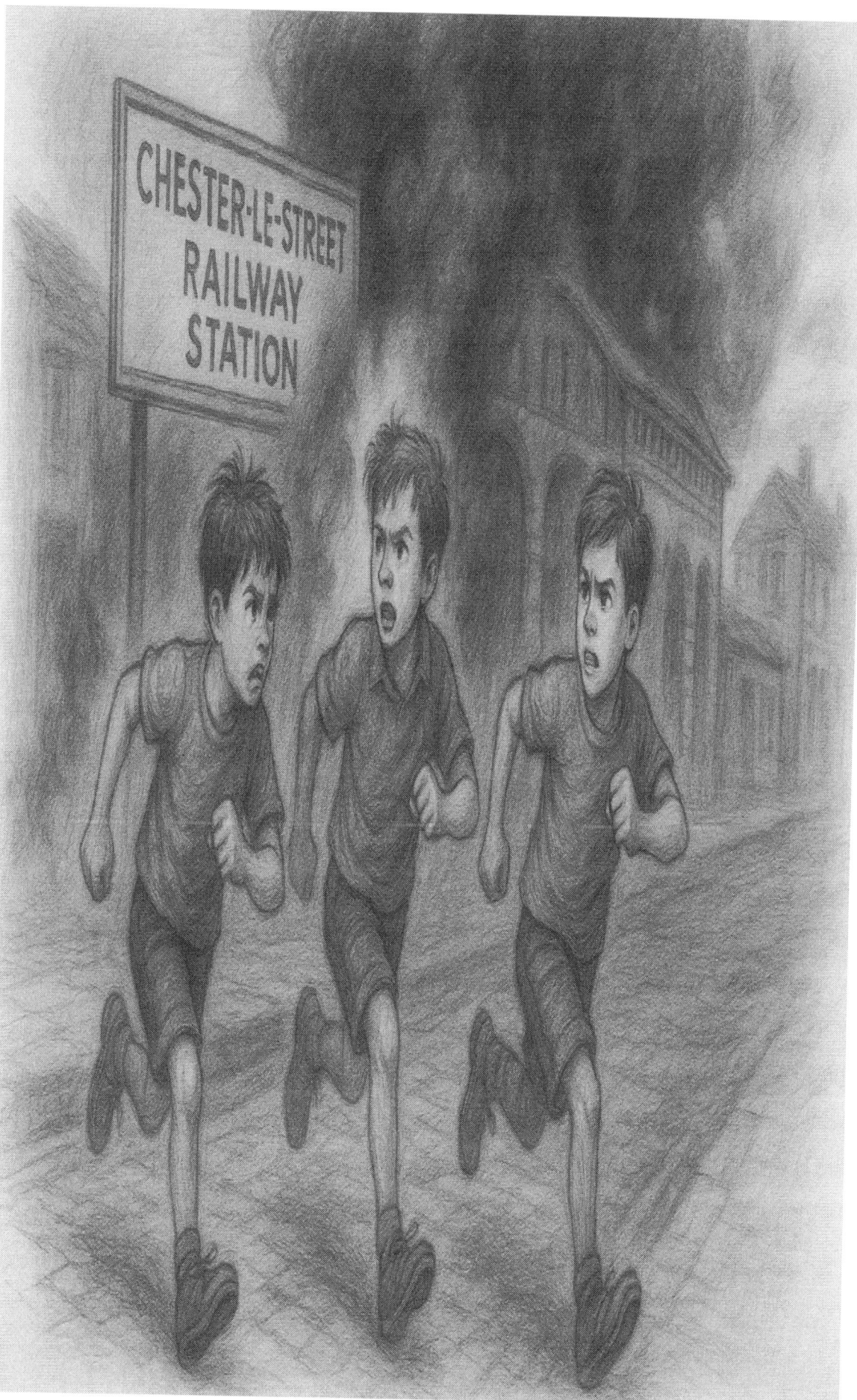

Me and Phill, Christmas morning at Deleval early 1970s

Below

Me, Phill, Mam and Sandy the dog at Deleval early 1970s

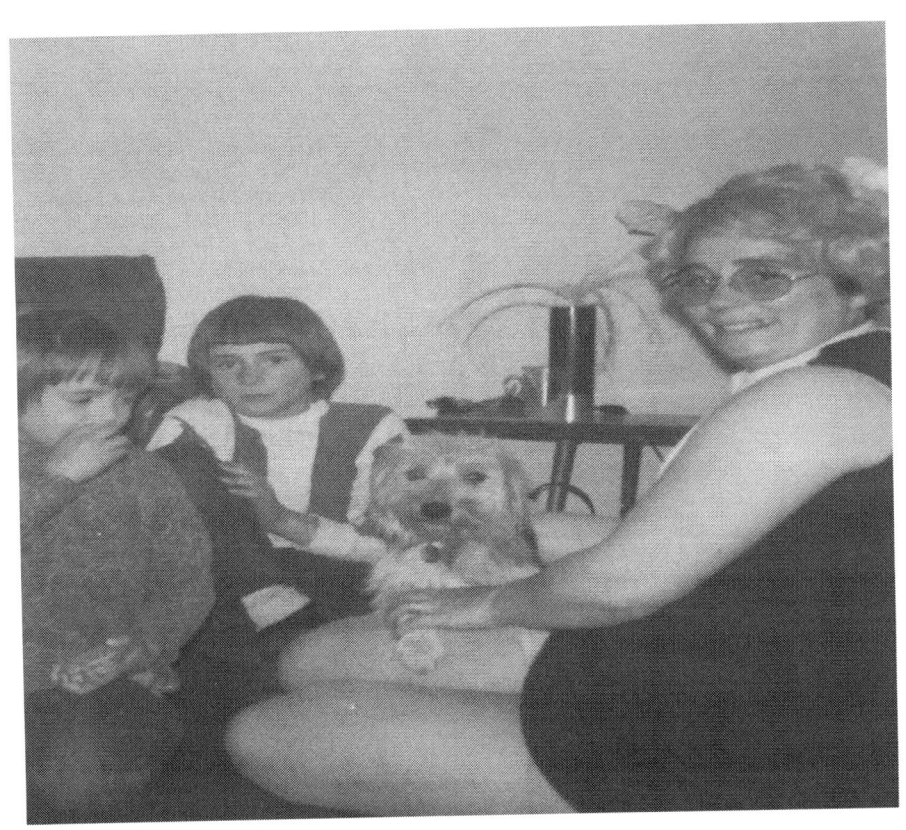

Chapter 10

The Commando Club

Like most young lads, I wanted to be popular amongst my friends and spent a considerable amount of time thinking how I could achieve it. I was rubbish at football and, to be honest, wasn't really sporty at all.

I had an idea — I'd start a club. As the clubhouse would be in my mam's garage, I'd automatically be the club leader. As such, I'd finally get the popularity I'd desired for so long.

This was just another silly idea I thought I'd never bring to life, so I pushed it to the back of my mind and got on with other thoughts.

It was Saturday, and Mam told me I had to go down Chester-le-Street as I needed a new pair of shoes. Most lads hated going shopping with their mams, but I loved it — she'd usually treat me to a chocolate éclair at a café called The Light Bite and some sweets and a comic from the newsagents.

We caught the 181 bus, and I insisted on going upstairs and sitting at the front as it made me feel important. We got off and visited several shops: Loughlens the butcher's, the fruit shop, the Co-op, and Greggs for a couple of stotties. Eventually, it was time to get my shoes.

Clark's was the shop in the middle of Chester-le-Street. It was a small shop with a slide for little kids. I always wanted to use the slide but thought I was a big lad and too old.

I chose a pair of shoes and did the usual walking up and down to check if they fitted.

"Yes, Mam, they're great!" I said impatiently, i just wanted to get my comic and sweets.

Then it happened.

"And you get a badge with these shoes!" the shop assistant shouted across the shop, coming over with a box of badges.

All the badges said the same thing: THE COMMANDO CLUB.

The shoes were hard-wearing school shoes for boys called Commando Shoes, and the badge was part of the promotion. That was it!

I picked my badge and watched as the shop assistant put the box back on the shelf. While Mam and the assistant chatted, I helped myself to several badges. I would be popular, I'd call my new club The Commando Club, and every member would get a free badge.

As soon as I got home, I got to work. Using coloured chalks, I drew a big letter C on the back wall of the garage. Yes you've guessed it, C for Commando.

Over the next week, I told all my friends about the club and the badges they'd get, and I announced a grand opening on Saturday afternoon — there'd be pop and biscuits too.

Saturday arrived, and the realisation hit me: I had no money for pop and biscuits. Then I had an idea.

We didn't own our TV as it was rented from Rediffusion. They made their money by charging 50p for every two hours of viewing, and when the time ran out, you just inserted another 50p into the coin box on the side of the TV.

I got a knife and used it like a mini crowbar to force open the coin box. Crash! Bang! It was open — and I had over £10 in fifty-pence pieces! There was a problem, though — I couldn't get the front back on the coin box. Never mind, I could sort that later.

I went down to the corner shop and bought two packets of chocolate biscuits and ten blackcurrant drinks — the type with the little straw you poke through the top.

When I got back, Neil Petrie and Neil Wilkinson had arrived. They helped me set up a couple of tables, put the biscuits on plates and line up the drinks. I proudly presented them with their club badges, which they pinned on their jumpers with pride.

The two Neils convinced me I hadn't bought enough biscuits and drinks, so I left them in charge while I popped back down to the shop for another packet of biscuits and another half dozen drinks.

I returned to find all the juice gone and the biscuits eaten. Neil Petrie and Neil Wilkinson had tricked me — the greedy pigs had scoffed the lot.

The Commando Club had ended before it had even begun.

It was school on Monday, and the Commando Club — along with the antics of the two Neils was the main talking point. Both of them wore their Commando badges, making things worse. What a day. I was a laughing stock. The day just couldn't get any worse… or so I thought.

I finished school and walked the short distance home. As I turned the corner, my heart sank. Parked on the kerb outside our house was the Rediffusion van, calling to empty the cash box on the TV.

I tried to go straight to my room, but Mam's voice screeched through the house.

"SEAN, IS THAT YOU? GET IN HERE!"

I opened the living room door and was faced with Mam and the Rediffusion engineer — Mam holding the front cover from the TV coin box. I looked down, trying to compose myself, searching for an excuse, but couldn't think of anything to say. All I could think was - What a cracking pair of shoes!

Me, (left) Colin Winter (centre) and Peche (Neil Petrie, right) on out first lads holiday to Blackpool 1983.

Below

Colin Winter (top) Me, (centre) Peche (Neil Petrie, holding us up) Chester le Street park 1984.

Chapter 11

Away with the Tide

It was the summer of 1976. I don't actually recall which day of the week it was — they all seemed to run into one — but I remember it was hot and sunny.

Nigel and I were both wearing trunks and t-shirts. Of course, I proudly displayed my collection of swimming badges, which Mam had stitched on my trunks ready for the summer holidays — 50 to 2000 metre swim badges, as well as bronze to gold survival awards. People would think I was part fish, and of course, I thought it might attract the girls.

But truth be told, I could hardly bloody swim. Those badges actually belonged to some older lad who'd dropped his trunks one night leaving Chester-le-Street swimming baths — and I'd made good use of them ever since.

Nigel and I spent the morning rock-pooling for crabs, turning over rock after rock looking for that giant one we were sure was hiding somewhere. By dinner time we'd moved around from Beadnell Point to Beadnell Harbour, by which time the tide was high.

We watched as some older lads in wetsuits were jumping from the buttresses of the harbour mouth. I hated people with wetsuits — their families obviously had money, or so I thought.

"You wouldn't dare do that," Nigel said to me.

"Neither would you," I shot back.

After a bit more daring and daft talk, we decided to have a go — but from the pier, where the drop was smaller even though the water was deeper. It took a while, but eventually, we jumped together. It was freezing — shocking, actually — but we couldn't wait to climb up those steel ladders and do it again.

We carried on diving and jumping for most of the afternoon until some divers turned up in a big rigid inflatable and started to moor their boat right where we were swimming.

"Out the fucking way!" one of them shouted.

"We were here first!" I yelled back.

"Fucking move or I'll give you a smack, you little shit!" he barked.

So we moved. They tied up their boat and walked off towards Harbour Road, where a van sometimes parked selling teas and coffees.

"Shitheads. They'll pay for that," I muttered to Nigel, grinning.

Then, laughing, I untied their boat — which was full of diving gear, air bottles, masks, and other expensive-looking stuff, not to mention a massive outboard motor, black with Mariner written across the top.

We slipped away to the other side of the harbour, where we could still see what was going on. At first, nothing happened — the boat just rose and fell with the outgoing tide. Then the rope I'd untied slipped off the metal ring and splashed into the water. Within minutes, the boat had turned sideways and was drifting — 50 metres out, then more — heading quickly out to sea. I was thrilled. My plan had worked.

We moved down onto the beach and away from the harbour, keeping an eye on the divers' boat as it grew smaller and smaller until eventually it was gone.

Of course, we weren't there to see the divers' faces when they came back and found their boat and all their kit missing. But that didn't matter. As far as we were concerned, it was a victory — revenge for them spoiling our afternoon fun.

"You two must've smelled the fish and chips," Dad laughed as we walked into the caravan.

"What have you been up to?" Linda asked.

"Just crabbing," we said in perfect unison.

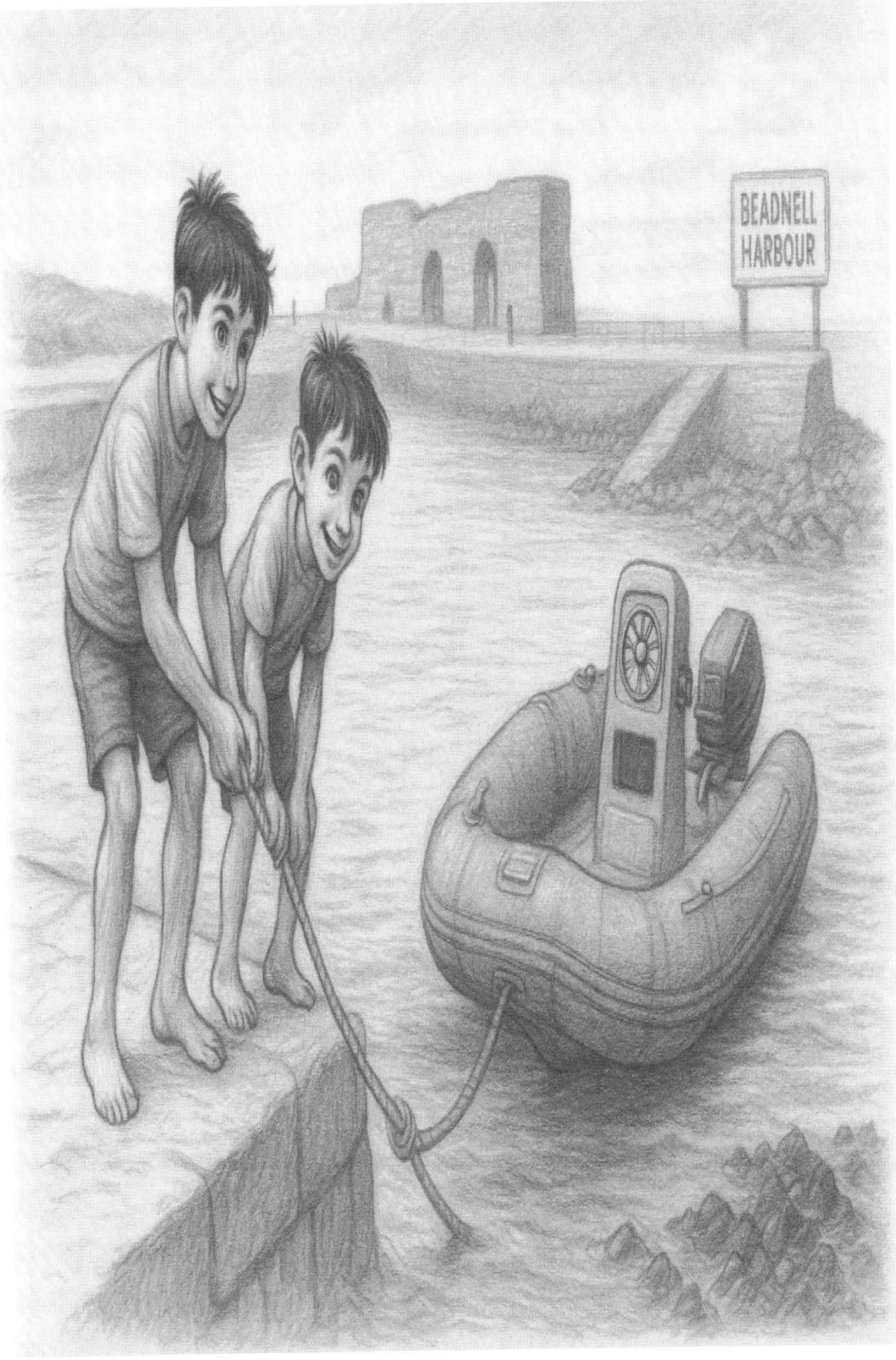

Chapter 12

The OUIJA Board

In 1977 my Brother Phill acquired a big black book all about Satanism and on the front cover it had a picture Pentagram and inside the story of Devil Worship, Witches, pin dolls and poltergeists, just the look at the book cover made the hairs on my neck stand up.

I would take the book out to my friends house and we would turn the pages slowly amazed at the photos and drawings of Satin and ghosts caught on camera.

One particular chapter concentrated on methods of how people could contact the dead. Peche, Colin Winter and myself read with interest and fear.

At the top of 3rd Avenue lived a lad called Gary Huntley, We let Gary see the book, "That's rubbish" he said. This wasn't what we wanted to hear as we loved looking at the book it gave us a thrill just like the feeling you get when you heard a good ghost story. We hatched a plan!

" Well if you think it's rubbish you won't want to come to the seance we are having tonight"

"What's that?" Gary asked" I explained it was a way of contacting the dead. Gary's eyes grew wide as if the ghost was right there in front of him. "Yes, can I come lads"

"Ok, mam goes to work at 6pm. Come round to mine at 7:30pm and we will contact the dead."

I wasn't lying, mam did go to work at 6pm. Once she had left, Peche, Colin and me got to work taking ideas from the book. We cut out bits of paper and wrote the alphabet in capital letters on each piece, placing these in a circle on the dining room table, I found a roll of fishing line in my brothers room and carefully got to work tying the line around ornaments, curtains and a brush which stood in the corner.

7:30pm arrived and Gary arrived along with his sister who was a few years younger. We told Clair she was too young but she went on and on until we said she could stay.

The curtains were drawn and only the light from a side lamp eliminated the dining room. We all sat around with our fingers pressed on an up turned glass in the middle of the table.

"IS THERE ANY BODY THERE" I shouted, the glass started to move towards the alphabet carefully placed around the edge of the table.

"That's you pushing it" Gary shouted, but we all denied it Gary wasn't sure and Clair didn't know what to think, D E V I L the glass spelt out. I pulled on the fishing line tied to the broom in the corner, it came crashing down, Colin pulled his and a ornament flew off the shelf, Peche pulled his and the curtains flapped open. Colin, Peche and me all jumped up and ran out the dining room shutting the door behind us, locking Gary and Clair in the dark room. We held the door shut so they couldn't get out, but realised we had gone too far when Clair started to cry and Gary screamed and shouted at the top of his voice. Of course we let them out and told them it was a joke, but that didn't matter as we had gone a little too far.

We laughed about it for the rest of the night. When I decided to go back in the house mam wasn't back and my brother and sister were still out, I was in the dining room clearing up the mess we had made.

I thought I heard a noise , I wasn't scared we had just been messing about, it was all rubbish just like Gary said. Nevertheless I thought to myself maybe it might be a good idea to put that book in the garage

Chapter 13

Pud and the Durex

There was a lad called Pud who lived in the street next to ours. The street was called Pinky Bank — or that's what we called it.

From time to time I'd knock about with Pud. He was a bit different from the rest of my mates — tall, ginger hair, and seemed a little posher and a little smarter.

It was a windy, cold Saturday afternoon and I'd gone to call on Pud. It turned out his mam and dad had gone out, so he invited me in.

I loved going into other people's houses — it was something different, and I was always hoping I might get the chance of a chocolate biscuit. We only ever had custard creams, and they didn't last two minutes in our house. Pud's parents were posh, so there might even be a mint Viscount. Mmmm.

We sat watching Saturday TV for a while, then Pud disappeared and came back with a couple of balloons. Only they weren't balloons, they were johnnies or condoms, if we go by their proper name. Pud's dad worked for Durex.

"Where are they from?" I asked.

"It's me dad's stock," Pud explained, throwing me a big handful of little packets.

I knew instinctively what to do. We both got to work blowing up dozens of condoms. Within fifteen minutes, the sitting room was full of inflated johnnies.

Outside, it was blowing a gale. We opened the door and started throwing them out into the wind.

We expected them to fly off gracefully, carried away into the sky like balloons at a fair. That didn't happen. Instead, about thirty condoms swirled around the garden, over the wall, into next door's yard, into their next door's yard — everywhere.

Before we had a chance to grab them, we heard Pud's dad's voice booming from outside.

"Pud! Are you responsible for this?"

Pud just nodded. His dad pointed sharply, and me and Pud instinctively started running around trying to catch the flying johnnies as they bounced around the garden like rubber ghosts.

I didn't see Pud much after that. Apparently, his parents thought I was a bad influence. Well, what did they expect — keeping boxes of johnnies in the house Since the fire at the railway, Pud's parents hadn't liked me much anyway, and could who could blame them.

Chapter 14

The Tent

It was sometime in the 1970s and I'm guessing we were around twelve years old.

It was the six-weeks summer holidays, and Neil Petrie, Colin Cowan and I decided to head up to Waldridge Woods.

In those days the walk to the woods seemed such a long way — well past the boundaries of the council estate where we lived and, to us was deep into the countryside. We set off with the intention of climbing trees and building camps.

On the way we stopped at Johnson's Farm to buy a bottle of milk each. It was a hot day, and we sat on the grass outside the farm gates drinking our milk. Refreshed and ready for adventure, we made our way into the woods.

We worked our way down to the middle where we crossed onto Butterfly Island by balancing on a fallen tree that made a natural bridge. Butterfly Island was a piece of land where the river forked and then joined again, leaving the ground in between completely surrounded by water.

To our surprise, someone had pitched a huge house tent on Butterfly Island. We ducked down and hid in the bushes, whispering about who it might belong to and whether anyone was inside. After a short discussion, we decided the best way to find out was to throw a few pebbles and see if anyone came out. Several well-aimed stones landed perfectly on the roof of the tent. Minutes passed — but no sign of life. We decided to approach.

Peche slowly unzipped the big front door and crawled inside.

"No one here!" he shouted.

He reckoned the tent had been abandoned, and we all agreed. Then came the idea that it must be worth money. So, with visions of riches in our heads, we decided to take it down.

It took a while, but the three of us worked hard, carefully removing every peg and pole until the whole thing was neatly folded and rolled up, ready to take back to Peche's house.

We struggled across the fallen tree, up the hill from Butterfly Island, through the woods and onto Waldridge Lane. We even passed the farm — so far, so good. no one had spotted us.

We carried on for about a quarter of a mile, arguing constantly about who was doing most of the carrying. In the end, we decided it wasn't worth the hassle and flung the tent into a field drainage ditch. That was that.

I often wonder what became of that tent — and what the poor people must have thought when they came back to find their pride and joy gone.

Chapter 15

Dallas and the Wallpaper Paste

It was 1980, and we were off school for the Easter holidays. I spent most of my time playing games in the street with my mates — Neil Petrie, Neil Wilkinson, and Colin Winter.

Bulldog, Kerbie, football, and mini-Olympics were just a few of the games we enjoyed. However, my love for street games had recently been surpassed by my love for the new American TV drama Dallas.

I'd been out all afternoon playing mini-Olympics but left around 6 p.m. to have a bath and get ready for Dallas. That particular night I had the house to myself — Mam was still at work at Chester-le-Street Hospital, where she worked as a nurse, Lesley was at her boyfriend's house, and Phill was out with his mates.

After my bath, I was making myself a couple of pieces of toast when there was a knock at the door.

When I opened it, it was Neil Petrie and Neil Wilkinson.

"Come on, are you coming out? We're going to do the Grand National!"

The "Grand National" was a race over the back garden fences from the top of Third Avenue to the bottom of the Crescent — smashing through cold frames and destroying people's plants, flowers, and vegetable patches in the process.

We did it from time to time, but I hated it because I wasn't as fit as the two Neils and always came last. Plus, the summer before, I'd caught my neck on a low-hanging washing line and nearly hung myself.

"I'm not doing it," I said. "I'm stopping in to watch Dallas."

Shit. I'd told them my secret. I liked Dallas.

"Dallas?!" they shouted. "Are you a puff?"

"No, it's good! And I'm not coming out!" I said, slamming the door.

That was that, or so I thought. I settled down in front of the telly to watch Dallas.

Two minutes in, I heard tapping on the window. I knew it was them but ignored it. The tapping turned into banging, and then I heard the sound of feet scrambling up onto the garage roof.

I ran upstairs and peeped out from behind the net curtain. In the dark, I could just see their shapes on the garage roof, throwing stones at the dining room window. I had an idea.

Mam had been wallpapering earlier, and there was still a big bowl of wallpaper paste in the kitchen. I opened the drawer and grabbed a soup ladle.

Very quietly, I opened the back door. I could see their shadows on the wall — the perfect targets. With the bowl of wallpaper paste in front of me and the ladle in hand, I launched my attack, scoop after scoop.

"What the fuck? He's throwing eggs at us!" Neil Wilkinson shouted.

They both scrambled down from the garage roof — covered head to toe in wallpaper paste.

"Me Mam'll kill us if I go back like this!" Neil wailed.

After a lot of persuading, I let them in the house to clean up. But once they were in, I couldn't get them out.

"Please, lads, go home — me Mam'll be back soon," I begged. They just laughed.

Ten minutes later, I heard the front door open. Oh no — Mam was home from work.

"HELLO, MRS SWEET!" they both shouted in unison.

"What have I told you?! OUT!" she roared. Off they went, laughing their heads off.

Mam wasn't speaking to me — and I'd missed Dallas. Still, there was always next week's episode.

Our house at Deleval

Below

Me and Sam the dog outside Dads house in Lowfell

Chapter 16

The Essoldo

On Chester-le-Street Front Street in the 1970s and early '80s, there stood an old cinema called The Essoldo. It had closed in the 1960s and been boarded up ever since. As you can imagine, a boarded-up building like that was a magnet for young lads who wanted to explore.

School was due to break up for the summer holidays in 1977, and a few of us made plans to get inside the Essoldo. We walked around the building looking for a loose board, but couldn't find one. Colin Cowan said his dad had a crowbar in his shed and ran off to get it.

When he came back, we managed to jemmy one of the boards loose and crawl through the gap.

We couldn't believe our eyes. Everything looked untouched — plush velvet seats, ornate plaster coving painted gold, and a huge red fire curtain that must've once risen and fallen for every film. It was fantastic. We explored the projection room and the ticket office; it felt as if everything had just been left the day it closed.

Over the next few weeks, we made the place our playground. We set up rope swings — one hanging from the upper circle down to the stalls, and another across the stage. It was brilliant.

But soon, word got around. Other kids found our way in, and before long the once quiet, forgotten cinema was full of children of all ages, running wild. The beautiful old building started to take a beating.

One Saturday afternoon we went back as usual, ready for a bit of swinging and exploring. But this time, someone had started storing bales of hay on the velvet seats.

Neil had a box of matches.

"Hey Sean," he said, "me and Colin will try to hit the bales with matches — you go down the bottom and put it out if it catches fire."

So I did — only, the thing was, I loved watching the way fire spread and changed things. So instead of putting the flames out, I was actually lighting the bottom of the hay bales myself.

Within minutes, smoke was everywhere — thick and grey, rolling across the stage and up toward the ceiling. Then we saw it: plumes of black smoke pouring out under the cinema doors, drifting onto the Front Street where people were out doing their Saturday shopping.

Soon, we heard it — the siren of a fire engine, We scrambled out through the entrance hole and legged it up Bullion Lane. From there, we could see the black smoke rising high above the rooftops. Thankfully, the fire brigade got it under control quickly and the cinema was saved.

By the time I got home, Mam could smell me before I even opened the door.

"You stink of smoke — and your face is black! You little sod, I knew that black smoke would have something to do with you!"

The council wasted no time after that. They had the cinema properly secured, and we never went back.

But less than two weeks later, the Essoldo burned to the ground — this time for good. A group of older lads, friends of my brother, were caught and sent to borstal.

We'd been lucky. but my fascination with fire had not been extinguished.

Chapter 17

Kermit and the Copper's Boot

From time to time in the early 1980s, Chester-le-Street Youth Centre would host all-night discos — usually arranged by Max, the manager, in an effort to raise much-needed funds.

Of course, we loved these discos. It was an excuse to stay out all night and get up to no good without our parents asking where we were.

In 1983 came the big announcement: Michael Jackson's Thriller video would be premiered on MTV. Max, never one to miss a fundraising chance, organised another all-nighter built around the screening.

Loads of us bought tickets — me, Peche (Neil Petrie), Vinnie Taylor, Baz and Spelk (Mark Atkinson), to name a few.

The night came and we all piled in. We danced to Madness, The Specials, and Bad Manners, and sat in disgust while others shook their heads to Whitesnake and Motörhead. We hated that music — called it Heavy Hippy Shit.

When Thriller came on the big telly, I thought it was my chance to sit beside Morag Troupe — the best-looking girl I'd ever seen. But Colin Cowan had beaten me to it. What could I do? I asked her friend Julie Warmsley to ask Morag if she'd be my girlfriend.

"Are you fucking joking?" she shouted. "Put it this way — would Miss World go out with Kermit the Frog?"

I was devastated but tried not to show it. Fighting back tears, I watched the Thriller video along with everyone else. When it ended, to take my mind off being compared to Kermit, I persuaded Peche to set off a smoke bomb he'd pinched from Mr Hunt — the one he used in his greenhouse to kill pests.

Peche sneaked it into the dark corner of the disco room — right where the heavy metal fans were headbanging to the Heavy Hippy Shit. The smoke was unbelievable. It caught your throat straight away, and soon thick white clouds were pouring out the double doors and into reception.

Everyone evacuated, the fire brigade arrived, and once they found the cardboard tube of the smoke bomb, they knew it was us.

"You're out! Barred!" Max shouted, and threw about a dozen of us out into the night. It was about 3 a.m.

Vinnie Taylor produced a handful of party hooters — the sort that usually unfurl like a long snake's tongue when you blow them, except these didn't have the long bit. No one asked why he had them. We all took one and blew them like an orchestra of twelve mouth organs. What a racket.

We marched up behind the shops toward the cinema. A police car came round the corner — the coppers got out.

"Stop that bloody racket now!" one shouted.

They asked what we were doing out so late, we explained, and they told us to get home — and if we blew the hooters again, we'd be locked up. No problem, we said. They drove off. They hadn't gone 200 yards before we all instinctively blew the hooters again, as loud as we could.

"LEG IT!" someone yelled as the cop car screeched into reverse. Everyone ran towards Murray Road.

I had a plan — they'll get caught, not me.

I darted behind Nuttall's the cobbler's and crouched behind some bins. My heart was pounding so loud I was sure the cops could hear it.

Then I heard a van pull up. Doors opened, closed.

Shit — the dog van.

"Come out or I'll let the dog off!" a voice barked.

I crept out from behind the bins and suddenly felt an almighty pain as a copper kicked me right up my arse.

"Now get home, you little shit and tell your mates we know who they are!"

My arse was killing me, but it was better than being locked up. As I walked home, sore and sulking, I thought about the night. My backside and my pride were battered but still what a cracking night!

Old friends

From left to right, Craig, Peche, Spelk and me.

Spelk enjoying

Festival at Chester le Street

Me and Craig Blackpool 1984-1985

Me, Spelk and Peche late 1980s

Chapter 18

Cherry Tree Road and the Washing Machine

Sometime in the 1980s, probably around July 1984, I'd moved into a flat on Cherry Tree Road that my sister Lesley had bought. I lived there with her and her boyfriend, John.

It was a nice modern first-floor flat, well decorated and furnished. The only downside was the kitchen, far too small to fit in a washing machine. Lesley had found the perfect solution: stick it in the bathroom airing cupboard. A plumber ran an inlet pipe, and soon it was all plumbed in. The only catch was that you had to hook the drainage pipe over the bath and wedge it between the bath side and the grab handle.

One Saturday afternoon, I was getting ready to go out with my mates for a few beers. Shaved, showered, dressed — I was ready to hit the pub. Just before leaving, I remembered to put my work clothes in the wash. "Two seconds," I thought, and then I was gone, strolling down to the pub without a care in the world.

Fifteen minutes later, I was sat with my mates, pint in hand.

A few hours went by. During a chat, someone asked where I was living.

"Living at me sister's — Cherry Tree Roa— SHHHHIIIIT!" I shouted, jumping up from the table. I'd forgotten to put the bloody pipe over the bath!

I bolted out of the pub, hailed a taxi, and was back at the flat within minutes. My mind was racing — what was I about to find? Water running down the stairs? Suds filling the sitting room?

I opened the door, heart pounding. Nothing. The carpet was dry. I ran upstairs — still nothing. No water, no bubbles, no disaster. What a relief.

Just then, the door opened. It was John, Lesley's boyfriend.

"What's up with you?" he asked.

"You'll never believe it," I laughed. "I put the washer on without putting the pipe over the bath — and not a drop of water anywhere! Ha ha ha!"

"You're bloody joking," he said. "A single wash uses about thirty gallons of water — so where's it gone?"

We opened the door to the airing cupboard where the washer lived. Still dry. We pulled it out — and there it was. Behind the machine, the drainage pipe had slipped between two copper pipes that ran down into the flat below. We looked at each other in horror.

Downstairs, the bloke who lived below us Steve was a decent lad. I doubted he'd be cheerful once he saw what had happened.

Moments later, we heard his door slam and his voice echoing up the stairs:

"What the hell…?"

Then came the inevitable knock on our door.

"Do you know it's raining in my spare room?"

We went down to see the damage — and it was bad. His spare room ceiling had collapsed. The wallpaper was hanging off the walls, the carpet was two inches deep in soapy water, and all his clothes in the wardrobe were soaked through.

We claimed on Lesley's insurance, and Steve's flat was fixed up in the end — but I never forgot the dangers of washing machines after that.

THE END

…Okay, not really the end.

Life carried on, adventures continued, and new memories followed.

Printed in Dunstable, United Kingdom

74769330R00042